Brown Bears

Trace Taylor

Colors

Do you see the bears?

This is what bears can look like.

The Bear Family

This is a baby bear.

This is a bear mom.

Cubs

Baby bears live with the mom.

This bear has lots of baby bears.

Habitat

Bears live in the mountains.

Bears live in the forest.

Bears live in the snow.

Bears look like where they live.

Camouflage

This bear looks like the trees.

This bear looks like the sand.

This bear looks like the rocks.

Omnivore

A bear has to eat.

This bear will eat fish.

Moose

This bear will eat moose.

Caribou

This bear will eat deer.

Snowshoe Hare

This bear likes to eat rabbits.

Blueberries

This bear likes to eat berries.

Walnuts

This bear will eat lots of nuts.

Moths

This bear will eat lots of bugs.

Dandelions

This bear will eat flowers.

Competitors

Gray Wolf

Wolves eat what this bear eats.

Cougar or Puma

Cougars eat what this bear eats.

Scavengers

Bald Eagle

The eagle eats what this bear had.

Maggots/Fly Larvae

Bugs will eat what this bear had.

Brown Bears Live Here

Brown Bear Body Parts

29

The Brown Bear's Food Web

Carnivores and Omnivores

Herbivores

Plants

This Is How Energy Flows

Power Words
How many can you read?

a	has	live	see	to	will
can	in	look	the	what	with
do	is	lots	they	where	you
had	like	of	this		

Practice With National Reading Standards

1. What was this book about? How do you know? (CCSS 1)

2. Do brown bears only eat animals? What in the pictures and/or the words supports your answer? (CCSS 7)

3. Why do you think it helps brown bears to look like the places in which they live? What in the pictures and/or the words supports your answer? (CCSS 7)

For more information about the **National Reading Standards**, please visit www.americanreadingathome.com/common-core-standards